echo & lightning

poems

sheila packa

wildwood river press
duluth, minnesota

Also by Sheila Packa: *The Mother Tongue*

Echo & Lightning
(expanded edition)
© 2010 Sheila Packa
All rights reserved.

ISBN: 978-0-9843777-1-8

Library of Congress Control Number: 2010935470

Wildwood River Press
1748 Wildwood Road
Duluth, MN 55804

www.wildwoodriver.com

Acknowledgments: "The Circle I Draw" appeared as Circle in *Main Channel Voices*, Spring 2008. "Incantation: Muse" appeared in *Touchstone*, Summer 2008. "Confluence," "Fiddleheads" and "Twelve Tone Geese" appeared in *Trail Guide: Northland Prints and Poems*, c2008. Many of these poems have previously appeared in *Fearful Journey, Echo & Lightning* (chapbooks) and *Undertow,* (an audio CD) published by Wildwood River.

In gratitude to the Arrowhead Regional Arts Council and the Loft McKnight Fellowships for past financial support.

cover design by Kathy McTavish
text set in Minion Pro
visual art © Cecilia Ramon www.ceciliaramon.com

to Kathy and the cello

I

II

III

I

dream

two wild swans
came in the dark hours
by star light far into the journey
to lend their wings

traveled north over ten rivers
flew over moss riven
boulders broken from the mother stone

over the fens
and spears of birch
through the wordless
winds and migrations
flew over graves
and lovers reaching blindly
through sheets of northern lights

two swans with feathers of falling snow

twelve tone geese

in synchrony and angles

across forests

over rivers

below Venus or

clouds invisible borders

carrying nothing

besides star memories

along arteries of the body

into dark interiors

through the moon's phases

calling to each other

on lovers' endless roads

north and south

if you answer
when you hear their call

the geese in loose and shifting lines
from land to sea to cloud

cross the evening sun red
on clouds of plum
over rivers inlaid in gold
upon the slopes

over borders
if you need to leave

in every country
we are born to the same body

wind inimitable
invisible forces change us
beyond reach

if you make the sky your home

—it isn't easy, you can't bring
those things—

wrap in those lines
cross with them

a journey yes

wind turns the body
and ground falls away

geese unafraid of silence
or empty sky
must go must go must go

reach into the wind
move as clouds rimmed with sunlight
or dark cloud of rain

need to follow their flight
like ice in the spring
that once held the river

light surges in the veins
searches for the beginning
of a journey yes

music you haven't heard
didn't know you needed
opens deep

love root, silk thread

let me give enough of myself away
let me hold nothing so close
I can not release it.....

like breath that comes into the body
the way water leaves the shore
like love you've spent

the warmth of the shoulder
what softens the face
or gathers behind sorrow

gravity that presses its light inside
what doesn't resign in its reaching
but pauses for breath

a deep and awkward question
what is sealed in its tomb
what gains in its diminishing

let me keep nothing back
not the dead
not the broken seed cases
torn letters

love breathing in the palm
as I tear at the earth
not the vine, root
relinquished blossom

not the broken pot
shattered mirror, not the stone
the promise or rose
give it all—all

raspberry canes

ending is certain but changing
uses a landscape in wonder

wanting to cross or go over
rise from the beginning of things
take what comes as far as possible
find strength and lend it

with limits but heedless
in the slash amid tangles and thorns
with hand and finger and mouth

not lost but realizing a course
not of my own making
willing release into the hand of God
my life and what I could bring
steady wandering

gathering of me into things no longer
familiar or long lasting
no exit except from the body
these hands these eyes
rendering, drawing

a bloom worn by sun filled with rain
opened in deep passion
hung on the lattice of vine and leaf
not given to possessing
but unpossessing

released by an intersection
of friction and sunlight
as rain laden raspberries from yellow dry leaves
use both echo and lightning

thunder / perfect mind

hills echo
    in hills
thunder places in your hands
two skies
    rising sinking
thunder fills eye and ear
with shades
    of deep
colliding fronts
      inside
clouds speak
        the mind of stars
in constellation
    bodies
to give away
    the border
between sea and stones
or bones and light

to the wind

you come to clear the smoke
from the air and bring the altitude
of sky and birds

sweep away anxiety
dear wind you sing and howl
around the eaves

climb over the barriers
hold me in your give and take
you toss the trees violently

cross all boundaries at any velocity
come be easy dear wind
always in motion

hold me in the cradle
with the sound of your breath
in the tops of the waves

dear wind combing through the forest
and grass
searching with your body

rising at a front
be gentle dear wind
you enter every opening

I give you my ears my mouth my hands
so that you will fill and stir me
dear invisible perpetual

lover relentless one

threshold

in a fever I wrote her, erased her
found endless openings and fallings
in the net of language—uncertain music—

constructed from pen and paper
before the words, not after
re-arrange, delete the self

on the threshold of an empty page
push the heavy door
voyage out

swan

when music without melody
came in veils of northern light
curtains lifted or cloud in the crossing
when a vibrating
        body

turned my journey aside
made me threshold
pulled me from all the reaches
and I receded with no handhold

sky came in with a breath
shadow etched itself on stone
spoke a language opening to touch
when it was night and filled, bereft
afloat upon the planes of light

wolf moon / annunciation

I give myself up
what I was
whoever I was

life from life
attempts at flight

give my hours
blue arch of robes
to pass through gates

illumined by sun
whatever I was meant to be

my body
small bridge across time
a road traveled when
the life I was living went past

to become lost or bright
give my gifts

transfer tender ringing of stars
climb the ladder into night
fill my arms

center of fire

I come to you now
through the distance
without fear

wearing bracelets of fire
release my past
that burned with its bright life

ash drifts through the gate
on the road of wind
in wheels billows

falling into the world
upward and down
through the clouds

that take me into their changes
I come smudged by absence

dark with desire
for the invisible
body between us

below your palm
above my clavicle
for the center of fire

catching
emerging tendrils
flashes on the water

your face and corolla
your dawn
dissolve me

leda (version I)

no time to say good-bye, I—
broken glass, odd how some things never
moved and others never moored
in exchange I, a molten core

with unbearable pouring against
the panes, giving way finally to the body
not taken, given, I—I
in the mouth of god—

dark angels sing after night fall
lift grief into the golden rim of clouds
under a vibration
                        of wings grateful
for the aftermath of sun, for prayers
never answered

leda (version II)

to be untied, broken
from a constellation, let go
like a bow across the strings
to be chastened by the dark

bound by what doesn't reach
spilled, hounded by the need to
give in, to give what nothing
one has, a sound or

a vibration of waves for a force
that drove the waves in and turned upon itself
and drove them out as well
                    both heaven and hell
in exchange gave up food and sleep
the body's ribcage, whatever, not keep

gift (version III)

the body yes
but more than that
everything I had
and couldn't hold

faces that are gone
the nakedness of birth
its exertions
bound with cloth

worn and torn from another life
music pulled under
by its current
          in the night lake
dark with crimson
boat and bird and broken

ascent

I have found you
in late winter storms

in the rising of years
and come when you call

I have heard you calling
upon the sea where words

sweep like a net
through the moonlit

surfaces of water shining
like copper and silver implements

I have washed you in my hands
and hung the towels

unlocked the doors
opened the windows

when I heard your voice
went into absolute darkness

into a new atmosphere
climbed a staircase

of notes and ascended
the sky's road

crossed bridges of clouds
lit by dying stars

sky

sky swallowed a seagull
that walked through her body
white feathers grey
yellow eye
in a dark wave without bottom
that drowned in flight
clouds sieving the night
while the bird tumbled in depth
like a stone many stones
making for shore
moonlight and waves
wing over wing a language
for disappearing

blues / breakup

on the far edge
lake ice piles on shore
aqua stacks
on a zinc shelf
falls into other hues
breaks like eggshell
when it's time
breaks like a violent
accident of glazed bowl
shattered with pathways
depressions and bruises
in waves
with fathoms of sky
between fractures
blew as in wind
blue as in sea
as in body each
journey begins in
violet, wet
goes through rose, grey
ends in profusion
finds in each form
silver or sheer sagacity
not to give itself one name

II

(without bridge)

from a house made of bones
beating drum
dream from the marsh
fish eggs, cattails, dragonfly mating

from pouring
currents without bridge
lovers union
comes without corners

for the boatman
a coin of two sides
comes to standing waves
and rowing against force

(immersion)

water resists
breaks without breaking
flows along invisible scores
courses between continuous
ends, begins

doesn't resist
touches, touches, turns
over the same skin

body around my body
body of sky
        of iron
body of toss and turn
        of shallow and deep
body of broken things
        of mud and weeds
        of cold and heat
        of cells and sleep
body of bodies
body of minerals and salts
        of light and shadow
        of obsession
body of work, of play
        of sound
body of birds in flight

(hidden things)

beneath the surface more surface

folded memories
closed doors

beneath the blue nets
chains, reversals
a hidden precipice

electrical impulses
explosions

velocity resembling thunder
dissolving particles

waves
played by hammer and anvil
overtures, underscores

planetary influences
invisible tensing, flexing
releasing

simultaneous being, non-being
not erasing, annihilating

not replicating, creating

(between us we are a vessel)

in the hold of our bodies
we are rising and falling
unmoored adrift
I am the stem you are the stern
restraining releasing
our hands the masts
in our private motion
vibrant ocean

(strange symmetry)

in the concert
of surface tensions

the climbing wave, green water
uneven rising, falling
spilled terrain

places we traveled
on a keel of music pressed against
the body

what I wanted but couldn't keep
comes close, can not arrive

breaks against this ledge
falling deep into the sky

where sun and crescent
moon, little scythe, tremble
if I were to speak of

god, wind, water
or infinity's boat
the underworld displaces

a spray of stars
clouds of night cresting

(not stream but eddy)

not journey to another world

stairs
downward whirring of notes

reached by breath
deep emerald
hidden in the day
shadow of chance

hours never rising

bronze inside and rust

fallen leaves
fastened by movement

slow stones on the verge
of sand

ribs of the body asleep

(after)

you sleep after rapture, after the beat
of wings, confusion of hearts, you sleep
after conception and birth's exertion
never the same, broken and worn deep

you sleep after pushing, the nameless
already a long journey, wind in the reeds
and still you sleep in the submersion
of dream, strong propulsion, webbed feet

as if you live outside yourself, incomplete
in the waters of the lake, weave
of white lace and mud at the bottom
           of new life, your own
heart outside your body and a thirst
to draw from what you are pouring

(helpless)

the body submerged, covered
by leaves, fast currents, poisons, past rescue
the river relentless, stones rolling in the bed

the body in darkness, covered
by gods, fallen, speaking under water
this place, gone by tomorrow

seize what you can, if you come
to the river, listen, the voices of the dead
rise up like poems

(song / eurydyce)

when I sang in the underworld, a ladder of light
        descended
link by beloved link, encased in amber, a golden chain
to hold the submerged, drowned, released

a bubble of air climbed to the surface
without breaking, without me
when I sang it was the song of the lily
the sun, a song chiseled into stone, a song of cranes
landing on the beach in fog

when you come in your grief
and swim, dive into the wreck
you will not find what you lost
only this corroded coin, this weed
in the silence of a shrouded lake, no song at all

but driftwood, a plank broken from the boat
with a rusted nail, wave on wave as you emerge
        each day it goes deeper
becomes artifact or history, follows you

(shore)

it wasn't pain but waves
pounding on shore
rolling of small stones
up the slope and back
ungraspable
breaking waves
with their spatter of white foam
all night long re-living
that peak or pitch
recognizing reorganizing
tossing
building up and dissipating
all night long
it was the world
creating, recreating, retreating
and waves capitulating

(vigil)

heat now without body
left in the breath
light without bone

shadow without night
given for deep exchange
ache by ache

birds fly through her
empty hands and feet
now on her knees

cold without stars
anchored adrift
deep without sides

rain without reach
for rivers that either
hold or sweep

fall through her ribcage
fall from the sky
drift into sleep

(mouth)

the river comes to the sea
in the end everything
that has been spoken
falls in, waves
take in the pouring of a stream
endlessly muddy
forks and erosions, excursions
forward and backwash
in union, in deep
stones wear against stones
words cancel words
fish that have swum upstream
to spawn return followed by
progeny, followed by
stream beds, followed by
fishermen, followed by gulls
stirring the moon
on the naked back of the sea

(battering)

the sea, the sea
tosses fathoms

lifts light on its shoulders
lifts prevailing winds
to ride its grey fields

gravity relents its forces
as the sea shoves its weight

inside all that it hides
empties and fills the lungs

reaches over stones
pulls from underneath

takes weather below its crests
falls over clouds and flights

down by the pier
down by the harbor
down by the mouth of the river

up by the beach slapped flat
littered by wood and weeds

(displacement)

the long slow wave of the sea
doesn't break

comes full of lead or violets or ice
pulls stones

from a stone beach while the other world
cast underneath

rolls to the pier under vessels and gulls
bears down

pulls on the chains climbs over
islands

taking plates and windows into dark weeds
releases into sky's face

driftwood silvered bone rusted iron hinge
moon

tarnished clouds broken ends of bottles smoothed
into gems

the long slow wave of the sea
lifts from the other side or underside without cease

(what sea)

what sea
cast in the world
in falling nets
rises inside
with waves
shimmering
can break the confines
shifting bottom
stirring weeds
part its waters
when you need
to breathe or flee

(river begins)

river begins in the other world
without time—

begins, flows through the body
inside, its shore

river begins and begins (sky and sky
and sky)

each bend (knee or elbow) smoothes
the stone

joins the strands of over and under
and besides

given
its nature of never going empty

watercourse and delta
river begins

lifting you, taking the silt
finally you wear thin, fall in

begin as river
possessed by light

(invisible embrace)

all my life the one
like a star at night
in a clear sky
called me to its light
shimmered inside
against my ribs
dreamt inside my skin
or beside me
a trembling brimming
body where waves
concentric urges
a finger's touch begins

(nocturne / snow)

reaches into my body
exhales into wing

crosses rivers that split and divide
night and its dreams

falls into dark rings
black veins
roots' taut strings

in the half light
descends stairs without end

every day arrives
into the world changed

given to season or wind or age
disappears in the hand

in the next world received
rises from night's edge

comes through the gate
stretches the hour

white wingspan of light

(morning)

morning led me upstairs
into starlight
desire suddenly woken into music

morning was a door
in the wall of darkness
deep and down and a heat—

if she could but press her fingers
against my body to release it

morning walked
into another world
would never be home again

too much was the grief
for what I had not yet done or known
that maybe I couldn't

an ascension of longing I climbed
and reached

green shattered and fell
snow drifted and filled
spruce with blue shadow

clouds with clouds
grey and yellow edge

morning tore away, went under
broke

the ladder fell away

an hourglass extinguished
in the pouring
of water into night

morning of the invisible
morning of threshold and distance

(breaking light)

the harbor lights lose themselves in the sea
love with a careless combustion
float until extinguished by dawn

forgive them

the great lake murmurs in sympathy
comes to shore to soothe with a steady rhythm
as if a heart beat in its body

comes to breathe on the losses
our own dark absence

(hull)

holding the rain inside
I drift untied
silent companion to cloud unforming
first stern then aft
in circles half circles
empty of breath
strange compass without true north
frame for desire
lost or released
tracing the fire's flight
rope falling into weeds
bent grasses lily pads
pulling the deep
smell of seaweed fish guts pine needles
lifting in waves as blue heron
goes deeper between sun and sun
sky finally underneath

III

love never meant sky

love never meant sky to me
when each day was so much
like every day

before the flames rose
and past promises turned to ash

before love
when I turned to speak, everything was smoke
and we were fleeing
carrying things from the house

love never meant sky
nor did the stars mean fire

tonight the sunset caught me unaware
and I traced the extinguishing moments

like the fall
when summer ignites into orange
and crimson and yellow with first frost

love never meant sky
until I could not span the distance
            and the leaves
never meant fall
never meant fire

butterfly

The butterfly by the river
rises like the sun in the sky's bowl
climbing like heat or time
and falling. The world
isn't without seeing
both beautiful and brutal
not far. Nor does the fox
regret its path. We go
like a sheer cloud
turn where we didn't mean
to turn, get lost in no
dense thicket, without a foothold.
But that is grace, that is mercy.

fiddleheads

as if all winter
music was underground

as if the body submerges its rhythms
until snow becomes a memory

and light falls down
into desire
among the mosses
on soft ground into rhizomes

as if
the body could dream
of all the things it couldn't reach

as if first fiddleheads then
root strings
pressed by the fingertips
of everything lost or dead or buried

as if absence drew the bow across shadows
to play a sound
that lifted wings in the branches
and across the breach
springs flow

confluence

you were given to me
      and I to you
your river
      falling like breath or light
over stones, airborne
broken silver
      into the river of my own
I hear you falling
through
      the forest where no one goes
through crimson and evergreen and azure
tumbling in the deep bed
your currents braid with mine
tug upon the roots of things
covering and uncovering
      I take you with
      inside of me
feel your heart frenzy of wings
      reverberating deep tones
for the rain
      the sun
        the hills fall into us
and rise with a wild sound
weeping and laughing indivisible

the circle I draw

I draw on love soaring on a pinnacle of wind
the wing beat through the trees
the shadows black as black as purple iridescence

I draw on the crowns of trees
the sound of stones talking loneliness

I draw the ache from the broken heart
          that tears the light to ribbons
to carry it to the highest point to feed the darkness

I draw upon the dead
delicate lichen etched upon a face
the origin of ice, the wingspan, the burst of flight

I draw the deep thickets with animals going no one knows

I draw the raven around me twice

incantation / muse

in the north
in the rising of waters
in the rising over the sun over the lake
in the rising of wind
in the rising of storms and love, of hawks, of music
where the dark world turns on its axis
beneath the constellations we are born under
where the stars cast their light infinitely
where the clouds cast their shadows

muse,
with your body's strings, come
with your bridge across death, come
with your magic wands, come
with your ink stained breath
with your winged instrument
with the flicker of lightning behind closed lids
with the spark that flares with the smell of sulfur
        touch the wicks and ignite the body
with the silk threads that are spun in the cocoons
        weave your passion
with the flights of migrating birds
above the silver lakes and blue green forests
above the smoke of the houses
above the circulation of the highways
        lift me into the unfettered space
with your eyelash grant a wish
with your palm cupped against the cheek
        let the waters rise brimming
with your cheek against the breast
        let the waters come pouring

with your complete possession
    let the constant river come roaring
with your dreams made of star shine and smoke
with your music made of darkness and light

I come into your streams
I have untied myself
    let go of my fear
I have been giving myself away
    emptying myself for your gifts
I have prepared a home for you
    lit the stars, turned down the blanket of night
    come to meet you

salt / lot's wife

I align the salt and pepper
on the table between
the squares of black and white
as we separate
watch the geranium at the window
and the ice on the other side
grasp a cup, watch love go
into the salty street
between the black iron fence
and white drifts
around the street lamp
watch the unknown negotiations
of hot and cold
the old and new—
—don't look back

how long have I been a stone?

is it love if it can't dance
if it's a system of measurement
can love be an accident or a vision?
or a piece of music played by angels?

oh to be saved by angels

I climb the back of each string
each note pours a shaft of light
each note starts and stops my life
I ride upon a light horse
an indigo and graphite and platinum
and leafy and sky horse
ride the sound of rails
and nightfall
day break and the body

the body the body
one is made of wood
one is made of bone
one is made of light

oh to die and live in a house of light
pass through inviolate
turn caution aside

leaving was an act of love
turning an act of love

was there salt on the angel's tongue
when she told me to leave?
did she shake the house
trembling azaleas' red petals
against the green stems and leaves

every time I begin, petals fall
I am leaving or I've left
or one is leaving me
we are leaving still
edges brittle
some leaves are dead
some are green

what do you do without green?
what do you do with your lot?
what do you do without salt?
how long can you be a stone?

the angel rubs the bow
against the strings to make a fire
sparks fly into the billows

smoke rises
the cities are burning
she holds the strings down
on the other side, releases
fire from the ice
shadows come out of the trees
to feed Orion in the sky
she swallows the night
before she rises
the dark and salty night

following I make my own way
with the body
in confusion in the wilderness
in the place of tangles and shadows
and fallen trees up the hill
in the crossings
in the place of chairs and tables
on the mapless paper
through the past
in a story among other stories
make my own way
without an axe clear a path
toward the light of angels
leave the vanity and mirror

taste the salt on my face
where we were staying
I didn't want to stay
where we were going
I didn't want to go

look back, don't look back—

middle passage / mary magdalene

I poured the oil
to empty the vessel

(so much has been said)

and myself poured
until I was empty

like any woman
who needed an opening
to have a door, a solitude, a place
where I was alone

silence had a voice
that could be spoken for

would only give if I could give

would not speak
unless I sheltered it

the empty place
gave all I could

came and was not turned away

death the stone poured out
in the middle passage

where weight turned into light
and I was taken into language

the river falls

the river falls
over the edge
cascades over ledges

abandons itself
the river never
climbs backward

in time, nor reverses
does not relive
its beginnings or middles

along the grassy meadows
and stone banks
it weeps for

what it has known
but rushes forward
rejecting nothing

held the way
it needs to be held
the river might slow

but eventually sweeps
fills its bed
with its own splash

ripple tumble and flow
it wanders in the bays
and sways in the deep

fed by the rain
by other streams
the hidden springs

the river when it comes
time to fall—the brown river
red river white river—

never holds back at all

breaking into blossom

when a tendril extends
not a filament can be retrieved
not the stem nor its flower
nor its seed

nor the fire its ash
all fall into the wind and find
the deep ground dreaming

through winter and its blanket
the sleep of the trees
ice that holds the water still
        if only for a season

find what feeds the fire

lover and the wound of love

seed stem bud

breaking into blossom
must be painful
to tear the tight bud and flare
        in deep orange or red or flames

dusk

On her body
dusk. The circle of light
from the lamp falls on a pot
upon a round bowl
in front of the window

on her hips.
Roses bloom.
It's as if the light has found
a way to enter the body.

It's raining outside
and water flows into the vessels
and blossoms and out
on the umbrella
over the empty table.
On the lilacs.

It's as if music, as if light
plunged into the clouds
and the clouds wrapped
around its fists.

Green leaves all hearts
and stems like vines
and the light in the body
went into the roots
and the roots were sending it back.

As if we were wrapped
by clouds and rain
and in the center
darkness lifted.

falling star

when we were together
last night a star in the sky
fell into me
pulling the firmament behind

indigo and clouds
iron and hydrogen
burn inside, inhale

desire like a flame
in the place of my heart
from the constellation
where once I was fixed

frida's gaze

if I could gaze as unflinching
as wary or haughty or direct
at what comes

if I could see what feeds me
what waves are poised or roiling
or my heart
or hang the hummingbird
        for a pendant

or let the jaguar stalk
across my shoulder

if I could be so blind
and leave marks like these
if our hands could see, not to control
but to let go, or flow
into you or out or into the flames
of a fire that stains
the dark with light
the night with your dreams

if I could see the murder
the love with scalpels
and myself amidst the spectacular
country, the bloom and twist
the collision
the visitations

as if this pain could be accepted

graciously like gifts, generously
as if the mark were a stroke
that severed and swept

as if there were no choice at all, only givens
worn like thorns around the neck
as if the spine was a broken column
as if we all need a brace
as if, as if
in the capitulations and pressure

we've surrendered to the surgeries
      in tenderness

in the beginning

in the beginning was a note
before a word was written
along the lines against the sky
like birds that rest and rise up
and fly away

in the beginning was a note
before a word was spoken
written in rivers flowing
endlessly in the day and night
over stones and hard places

in the beginning was a note
before there was a word
written in the blood flowing
in the veins in the body
to places never seen

in the beginning was a note
in the limbs of trees swaying in the breeze
not silence exactly

into shore

into shore came driftwood
    fallen and polished
into shore came shattered and smoothed
    glass, translucent and blue
into the year came February
    cold and snow
into the storm came the other world
into the dead of winter came fire
into the keyholes, locks, into the hinged doors
    came relentless wind
into the wind, a music
    from the northern lights
into the scales, the shafts of solar dust
    lit by the departed sun
into the howling, an ecstasy
into the interior, immeasurable waves
into the battering, a sea
into the stones, slender green stems
into the cracks, love
into the vessel, into the body, the source

the calling

comes like notes
that press into my breast
into the chambers of the heart
and my blood takes it on roads

deep inside
that split and divide
it's never enough, what I have
in hand, the music...the circumference

goes beyond
the body (yours or mine)
the only thing that contains it
is the sky, sometimes by the stars

I can see
this other body
we're inside, the ribs' blue vault
and the wind coming in like breath

notes bend
around the strings
and turn like a river that rises and falls
along a landscape welling up in the twilight

petals
opening on white water
lilies and the crossing of bears
and winged migrations calling

from a tiny wire

from a tiny wire, vibrating
from far away, full of arrival, the wind

from the north smelling of permafrost
and smoke and sedgy marsh

sweeps down the latitudes and longitudes
drops degrees

drops water on the leaves
sun's relentless shining, unbroken
by cloud or wing or forest, drops

what the stars pick up by darkness
onward and endless
when the sky drops

shifting greens, yellow green, deep green
dark green, gray green, black and dust
star moss in the damp shadow of a tree

picks up the sound
white pine roots lift the flat stones
upward, everything into music

my love / villanelle

my love around you is a circle
I wrap you in blankets
I wrap you with feathers, with twigs

with wool, I wrap you
with leaves, with blues, with greens
my love around you is a circle

flights are ways of returning
with silver, with russet, with crimson
I wrap you with feathers, with twigs

let go to fall to the roots
let go to rise in the skies
my love around you is a circle

in sunlight and shadow, in music
with scales, with flows
I wrap you with feathers, with twigs

empty for filling
full for emptying
my love around you is a circle
I wrap you with feathers, with twigs

what's found

in the tangle of trees
in twigs
from branches
and trunks and roots
in the ephemeral
tenderness of green
leaves that last a season
in the trembling and wind
the blue of sky and lake
in clouds resounding
from a place of emptiness
a chamber that answers
in vibration, string and wind
a trembling, brimming and falling
in the place opposite of grief
the place opposite of dark
in the body of lost
in water and air
a star whose light
has ended but travels
toward us
rising and falling
in a cascade of notes
which is not endless
but aching and sweet
like iridescent feathers
of wings that rise and fall
in the circle of migration
in each flight
music that we breathe

love goes on

Love goes on in spite of the quarrels
    in spite of leavings, broken hearts, rejected rites
        discarded love letters, promises never kept
love goes on in face of all its failures
    betrayals, reverse in fortunes
        formidable opponents, competing needs.
Love goes on and on
    if not above ground then under, if not under
        then through, if not through
            then around, if not around, then over
and over, if not you, then another, if not
    another then another.
        Love goes on
            slips out of our grasp
                travels upon the roads
                    falls like rain and
floods and evaporates only to rain elsewhere.
Love goes on here and elsewhere
    beyond the bodies, the climax, the clasp
        of hand and mouth and ribs and limbs.
Love is beyond the pain of it, the disdain of it
    the stain of it, beyond the seed that falls
        beneath the soil before
            and after the rain that splits the seed open
            the tendril that lifts its small stem
goes on to leaf and back to seed.
Love is this circle that we're in
outside, inside, unsayable, unspeakable, unseeable
    unknowable creator and destroyer.
Love, love, love, how grief rises
    into dark stars.

what if a star

what if a star fell into your hand?
what would you do with the weight?
the infinite roaring
burning light?

what if a star fell into your hand?
what would you do without a body?
without shadow or distance
the end of night?

suspended in blue

Shore lifts as if breathing.
Inside the sky, origin of breath.

Blue strikes the horizon
while at my feet
water is cast in the chestnut tint
of yellow eyed ducks.
They swim in arcs.

Small pebbles unsettle the bottom.

The long heavy plank
of the past balances what's next
close by, in this moment

submerged, a silence—
too distant to see

an indigo reply
to what nobody can ask.

On the dock, tables
fill with diners looking out to sea.
In the marina, boats
lift and fall
on their ropes.

Beyond that, the vessel drifts.

A lighthouse, breakwater, mist.
No language for what blurs

lines, waves,
fathoms, invisible stars.

Echo & Lightning is one woman's love story, written for cello music composed by Kathy McTavish. This book is an expanded version of a chapbook of the same title, also included are many poems from the audio CD, *Undertow,* and the chapbook, *Fearful Journey.*

This work is about change. "Dream": The poem refers to lines from a Finnish poet, Helvi Juvonen. "I, a boulder split off the mother rock..." from her poem "The Boulder," translated by Keith Bosley. The title "Loveroot, Silkthread" is a line from Walt Whitman's *Leaves of Grass.*"Leda" (Version I and II) refer to Greek mythology, Leda and the Swan. "Thunder / Perfect Mind" borrows its title from the Gnostic text, *Thunder, Perfect Mind.* "Frida's Gaze" is about Frida Kahlo. Also referenced are three women in *The Bible* and their intersections with the divine (Mary, Mary Magdalene, and Lot's Wife) and the Greek myth of Orpheus and Eurydyce.

Sheila Packa is the Poet Laureate of Duluth, 2010-2012. The granddaughter of Finnish immigrants, she grew up on Minnesota's Iron Range. Her work, influenced by the Finnish language, explores the theme of migrations (of birds, grandmothers, and desire) and the natural world. She has published poetry, short stories and essays in several literary magazines, including *Ploughshares.* Her poems have been in several anthologies, including *Finnish-North American Literature in English* (Mellen Press, 2009) *Beloved of the Earth: Poems of Grief and Gratitude* (Holy Cow Press, 2008) and *To Sing Along the Way: Minnesota Women Poets from Pre-Territorial Days to the Present* (New Rivers Press, 2006). Poetry Harbor published her first chapbook, *Always Saying Good-bye.* Her book of poems, *The Mother Tongue* (Calyx Press, 2007), received recognition at the Northeast Minnesota Book Awards. She has received a Loft Mentor Award in poetry, two Arrowhead Regional Arts Council fellowships for poetry, a Career Opportunity grant, and two Loft McKnight Awards (in both poetry and prose). Some of the poems in this book are recorded with cello music by Kathy McTavish and are available as MP3s. For more information, please visit the websites www.cellodreams.com and www.sheilapacka.com.

CPSIA information can be obtained
at www.ICGtesting.com
Printed in the USA
LVOW12s1444181216
517833LV00001B/36/P